# Tides That Shape Us

# Tides That Shape Us

*Grief, the Language My Body Speaks Now*

Barry C. Eneh

RESOURCE *Publications* • Eugene, Oregon

TIDES THAT SHAPE US
Grief, the Language My Body Speaks Now



Resource Publications
An Imprint of Wipf and Stock Publishers
199 W. 8th Ave., Suite 3
Eugene, OR 97401

www.wipfandstock.com

PAPERBACK ISBN: 979-8-3852-7165-8
HARDCOVER ISBN: 979-8-3852-7166-5
EBOOK ISBN: 979-8-3852-7167-2

VERSION NUMBER 04/10/26

for the unseen, quiet champions who lifted us
when we could not yet see our own wings.

We came to the water carrying what broke us.
We left carrying what remade us.
Loss gave us its language;
light taught us its name.
What remained was not the wound,
but the widening
the quiet courage to belong to our own becoming.

# Contents

## MOVEMENT II—BREAKING OPEN (Listening)



## MOVEMENT III—BECOMING (Transforming)

**MOVEMENT IV—HOMECOMING (Returning)**

# Preface

## The Four Movements of Becoming

**Ache → Listening → Transforming → Returning**

Some seasons split the ground beneath our feet.
What once felt certain slips through our hands.
Love, identity, and belonging drift out with the tide.
What follows is not an ending,
but the beginning of another kind.

*Tides That Shape Us* was born from that ache
from the long apprenticeship of grief,
and the quiet revelation that sorrow is not only what we lose,
but what remakes us.

Each poem moves like water—leaving, returning,
reshaping the shoreline of who we are.

These poems are not answers.
They are invitations:
to pause, breathe, listen, and begin again.

Across its four movements—Loss, Breaking Open, Becoming,
and Homecoming
this book maps the interior geography of transformation.

It begins in fracture.
It travels through the in-between.
It arrives at the shimmering edge of wholeness
not as a return to what was,
but as an arrival into what is.

These pages are offerings:
for those learning to breathe again after loss;
for those who have crossed oceans of displacement and desire;
for those still waiting for language to find them.

They invite us to sit with the ache,
listen for the music beneath the noise,
and remember that healing is never linear.
It is tidal.
It is cyclical.
It is alive.

# Letter to the Reader

Dear Reader,

Thank you for opening these pages and stepping into this journey with me.

This book is a companion for anyone who has carried loss,
waited for clarity,
or searched for a way to return home to themselves.

As you move through these poems, take your time.
Return to what tugs at you.
Let the words breathe with you, shape you, soften you.

May these pages meet you where you are
and gently guide you toward where your soul is ready to go.

With tenderness,
Barry

# How to Read This Book

This book is best read slowly.

Move through each movement as if crossing a threshold.
Pause when a line holds you.
Reread what stirs something ancient.
Let the silence between poems do its quiet work.

You do not need to understand every word.
You only need to feel your way through.

This is not a book to finish
it is a book to inhabit.

# Introduction

## The Four Movements of Becoming

We do not become all at once.

We arrive in pieces
through rupture, through wonder,
through the ordinary moments that feel too small to matter
yet somehow change everything.

Every life, no matter how polished on the outside,
moves through four ancient movements:

## Break · Burn · Return · Become

This book was written from within that arc
from years spent beside hospital beds,
holding the hands of families in the soft hours when language breaks,
and from my own seasons of loss, disorientation, longing,
and unexpected light.

If these pages find you,
I trust they are meeting you in one of these movements.

Here is the map.

### Movement I—The Breaking

Where the old story cracks
and truth breathes through.

Breaking is not failure.
It is opening.

It is the moment the life you know
can no longer hold the self you're becoming.

In breaking, we meet the parts of ourselves
we once tried to outrun.

Pain is not punishment
it is invitation.

This is where the journey begins.

### Movement II—The Fire

Where surrender becomes strength
and the self is remade in quiet flame.

Transformation rarely arrives with fanfare.
It comes as refinement
burning away what no longer belongs
so you can gather the pieces of who you've always been.

### Movement III—The Returning

Where we find our way back
to breath, body, and belonging.

Returning is the soft work
of coming home to yourself
of remembering your worth,
your tenderness,
your place in the world.

## Movement IV—The Becoming

Where the self steps into its fullness
quietly, courageously, whole.

Becoming is not a destination.
It is a posture,
a way of meeting life
with an open spine
and an open heart.

## How to Enter This Book

You may read these pages straight through
or wander them like a shoreline.

Pause when a line catches you.
Reread what stirs.
Skip ahead when your heart seeks a different light.

There is no wrong door into this work.

This book is not asking you to be fixed
it is asking you to be found.

## A Final Word Before We Begin

Wherever you are in your story
breaking, burning, returning, or becoming
you are not alone.

The tide that brought you here
has more to teach you.

Welcome, traveler.
Take a breath.
A new beginning is already waiting in your hands.

## Sectional Map

**Movement I—Ache / Shattering**
The wound is named.
Grief. Disorientation. Fracture.

**Movement II—Tide / Holding**
Learning to stay with what hurts.
Language of water, tide, shoreline.

**Movement III—Fire / Becoming**
Refining, surrender, identity, courage to re-author the story.

**Movement—Homecoming / Beauty of What Remains**
Integration, gentleness, legacy, enough-ness.

# MOVEMENT I—LOSS (Ache)

## Movement I Opener

Loss arrives the way dusk does
not with permission,
but with presence.

It softens the edges of everything
you thought was certain,
teaching the body
the quiet weight of what once was.

Here, in this first darkness,
breath shortens, memory sharpens,
and the world becomes a room
you do not yet know how to inhabit.

But this is not abandonment.
This is initiation.

Before healing, there is naming.
Before naming, there is ache.
Before light, there is loss.

Enter gently.
Everything begins here.

## 1. When the Light Leaves the Room

When the light leaves the room,
it does not slam the door
it sighs.

A thinning of brightness,
a soft undoing
that teaches the walls how to weep.

You try to name the silence,
but it keeps shifting shape
a ghost in the doorway,
a breath you cannot hold,
a story still warm in the bed
you cannot bear to make.

People say loss arrives suddenly.
They are wrong.

Loss lingers.
It circles.
It studies your home for days,
touching everything you once loved
before choosing where to settle.

And when it finally sits beside you,
you do not scream.
You exhale.

Because somewhere inside,
you already knew
this moment was coming.

Grief is not the darkness.
It is the echo that remains
after the light has gone home.

## 2. When the Familiar Becomes a Ghost

There comes a day
you will know it by its stillness
when the familiar becomes a ghost.

Voices you trusted
unravel mid-sentence.

A chair still holds
the outline of the one you loved
but not their warmth.

Objects forget their stories.
Rooms forget your name.
Even your own reflection
hesitates to return your gaze.

This is the moment
the world blinks
and belonging thins.

Do not run.

Sit with the strangeness long enough
to hear what it knows:

Sometimes the soul must lose
what it once held tightly
to discover what it was born to carry.

### 3. The Day the Sky Forgot to Breathe

That morning, the sky forgot to breathe.
Clouds hung low, heavy with knowing,
as if they, too, were grieving.

Even the birds changed their song
their voices trembling
like someone praying
with a fractured faith.

You moved through the day
as though underwater,
each step a negotiation
between what your body remembered
and what your heart could no longer hold.

Some days grief speaks loudly.
Some days it speaks through silence.

But on that morning,
the whole sky carried your sorrow
so your chest wouldn't have to.

## 4. Before I Vanished

Before I vanished,
I left small clues
for the version of me
who would one day return.

A note taped to the mirror:
*Remember who you were*
*before the breaking.*

A prayer inside my shoes:
*Walk gently. The earth beneath you*
*is also healing.*

A whisper on my pillow:
*Your absence is not failure.*
*It is survival.*

I did not disappear.
I folded myself
into a quieter place
until I was ready
to be found.

## 5. What Loss Teaches the Body

Loss teaches the body
what language cannot bear.

Hands learn how to cradle absence.
Shoulders memorize the weight
of unfinished stories.

The spine bends
to shelter rooms
we cannot return to.

But the heart
the heart becomes a lantern,
glowing with a tenderness
the darkness cannot swallow.

## 6. The First Night Without You

The first night without you
was a study in hollowing.

The bed stretched wider.
The hours grew teeth.

The darkness pressed its ear
against my chest
to listen for something breaking.

Grief did not slip in quietly.
It climbed into the sheets,
curled itself beside my ribs,
and whispered,

*I will stay*
*until you listen.*

## 7. When the Sun Sets Too Soon

Some endings arrive early.
Some arrive twice.
Some never learned
how to end at all.

That evening, the sun set
before the day was ready.

Light spilled quickly,
fleeing the horizon
like a truth escaping.

And for a moment,
you understood:

Not every promise is meant to stay.
Not every staying
is mercy.

## 8. The Ache That Finds a Name

There is a moment in grief
when the ache finds a name.

It rises from the throat
like a trembling truth
you are finally willing to touch.

Speaking it
breaks something open.
Hearing it
unlocks something hidden.

Living with it
teaches you how to carry
what carrying cannot cure.

## 9. A Language Not Yet Spoken

Grief is a language
the body speaks
before the tongue learns how.

It tightens the jaw,
bends the spine,
pools behind the eyes
in unspoken sentences.

Only when the body softens
does the truth emerge:

*I cannot hold this alone.*

That moment
is the beginning of healing.

## 10. What I Couldn't Say at the End

I wanted to tell you
I wasn't ready.

That the story was unfinished.
That we had not yet become
who we might have been
together.

But the ending came quickly,
a tide that could not be negotiated.

So I whispered the only truth
my shaking voice could hold:

*Thank you*
*for every moment*
*I did not know how to cherish*
*until now.*

## 11. Your Silence Taught Me Everything

Your silence was a teacher
honest, patient,
uncomfortably sacred.

It showed me
that absence speaks
in complete sentences,

that love survives
even what it cannot hold,

and that some truths
only arrive
after goodbye.

## 12. I Prayed for Goodbye Before It Came

Here is the confession
I never meant to keep:

I prayed for goodbye
before it arrived.

Not because I wanted to lose you,
but because I could not bear
the slow unraveling
of your leaving.

Sometimes mercy
looks like surrender.

Sometimes love
is letting go
before the breaking
becomes cruel.

## 13. A Map of the Unsaid

There are places inside me
I never learned to speak from
rooms built of unfinished sentences,
hollow corners shaped by fear,
hallways echoing
with what I never dared to admit.

Loss has a way
of drawing the map
you spend your life avoiding.

But naming the unsaid
is the first step
toward bringing yourself home.

## Micro-Epitaph—Loss · Grief · Ache · Disorientation · Fracture

We let go.
We grieved.
We rose anyway.

**Reflection—Release · Grace · Renewal**

- What familiar ghosts still linger in your present life?
- Where are you holding on to a self that no longer fits?
- How has silence been a teacher for you?
- What does letting go make possible now?
- When the sky breaks next—how will you step through?

# MOVEMENT II—BREAKING OPEN (Listening)

This movement is where the darkness softens,
where grief loosens enough for breath to return,
where the soul begins to listen again.

The poems here shift from collapse to clarity,
from ache to awareness, from loss to learning.

## MOVEMENT II OPENER

Breaking open is not a violence.
It is an unveiling.

The heart does not shatter
it sheds its armor.

The body does not collapse
it remembers.

*There is a moment when the ache*
*you feared would undo you*
*becomes the doorway*
*to your own becoming.*

This is that moment.
Here, silence becomes a teacher.
Here, listening becomes a practice.
Here, you learn to stay present
to the truth you once outran.

Breaking open
is not the end.
It is the beginning
of understanding.

## 1. What the Silence Knew

Silence knew
long before I did
that something inside me
was asking to be heard.

It waited
patient as a held breath,
tender as a hand hovering
over a wound not ready for touch.

Silence is not empty.
It is ripe.
It carries the weight
of every truth
you're finally strong enough
to name.

When I was ready,
it didn't shout.
It whispered:

*Come closer.*
*There is something here*
*you must learn*
*to listen to.*

## 2. The Body Speaks in Grief

The body speaks
long before language does.

A trembling in the ribs.
A tightness behind the eyes.
A weight that settles
and refuses to leave.

Grief writes its messages
in muscle, bone, breath.
It speaks in shadows,
in stumbles,
in sudden stillness.

And when you finally listen,
you realize the body
was not betraying you.
It was telling the truth
you were not yet ready
to acknowledge.

## 3. Ghosts of Possibility

Every life you did not live
haunts the edges
of the one you chose.

Every version of you
that might have been
lingers like a soft echo
in the corners of your memory.

These ghosts do not accuse.
They remind.
They illuminate the paths
that shaped your becoming
even when you didn't walk them.

Possibility is never lost
it becomes the quiet teacher
guiding you
toward the life
you are finally ready
to claim.

## 4. When Healing Feels Like Losing

No one tells you
that healing sometimes feels
like losing all over again.

You look at the pieces
you've held so tightly
and realize
they no longer fit
who you are becoming.

Healing asks for honesty.
Honesty asks for release.
Release asks for courage.

And courage
courage asks you
to walk forward
without the weight
you once mistook
for identity.

## 5. Roots Beneath the Fall

When everything falls apart,
you discover the roots
you never knew you had.

Not the tidy ones
you show to the world
but the deep ones,
the ancient ones,
the ones that hold you
when your name dissolves
and your certainties collapse.

Falling is not failure.
Falling uncovers the foundation
you forgot was yours.

And from that ground,
everything begins again.

## 6. Saltwork

Grief is a saltwork
a slow purification
through tears,
through memory,
through the quiet burning
of letting go.

Salt preserves.
Salt seasons.
Salt transforms.

Your sorrow
is not a punishment.
It is a cleansing
a sacred alchemy
through which the heart
makes room
for what comes next.

## 7. When the World Goes Quiet

There comes a moment
when the world goes quiet
enough for you to hear
your own becoming.

Not the noise
of fear or expectation
but the soft hum
of truth rising.

Quiet is not absence.
It is arrival.
It is the sound
of your inner life
finally speaking
without interruption.

## 8. What Grief Asks of Us

Grief asks of us
what nothing else does:
to stay awake
to our own tenderness.

To stop running.
To stop numbing.
To stop pretending
that carrying it alone
is strength.

Grief asks for honesty,
for breath,
for presence.

Most of all,
grief asks us
to remain open
to the world
even after the world
has broken us.

## 9. Faith in the Dark

Faith is not the certainty
that light will return.

Faith is the willingness
to walk in the dark
with your hand
outstretched
trusting that something
will meet it.

Faith is choosing
to stay soft
in a world
that has given you
every reason
to harden.

Faith is breathing
even when your chest
forgets how.

## 10. Where the Rivers Go

Every tear
is a river
searching for the ocean
of your becoming.

Do not shame the flow.
Do not dam the current.

Let what breaks you open
teach you
the direction of your life.

Rivers know
where they're going
you just have to let them
carry you.

## 11. When the Sky Finally Breaks Open

There is a moment
when the sky breaks open
and you realize
you survived
what you thought
would end you.

Not with triumph,
but with truth.

You step into the air
and discover
you are still capable
of breath
and maybe even
of beginning again.

This is the threshold
between ache
and awakening.

Cross it gently.
Everything ahead
is new.

## Micro-Epitaph—Hurt · Tide · Shoreline

Break open.
Let the ache speak.
Light always finds
the honest wound.

### Reflection—Vulnerability · Truth-Telling · Bearing Witness

- What truth in you is asking to be spoken, even if your voice shakes?
- Which version of yourself are you still afraid to outgrow?
- How does your body speak what your mind silences?
- Where might your breaking be the beginning of something sacred?
- What does "light" mean to you now that you've seen the dark?

Movement II ends with a breath, not a conclusion. The voice quiets here, preparing for the transformation that follows in Movement III.

# MOVEMENT III—BECOMING (Transforming)

This movement is where grief no longer only breaks
it begins to *shape*.

Where silence becomes clarity,
where tenderness becomes strength,
and where the fractured self discovers
its own capacity to rise.

Here, your voice turns from mourning
to meaning.

## MOVEMENT III OPENER

Becoming is not becoming someone new
it is remembering
who you were
before fear taught you to shrink.

It is the slow gathering
of the parts of you
that grief scattered,
the gentle reassembly
of the self
your soul has always recognized.

Here, courage is quiet.
Transformation is subtle.
Light returns
one breath at a time.

This is the movement
of reorientation
of learning to live
with everything that shaped you,
without letting any of it
define your horizon.

*Becoming*
*is the art*
*of returning to yourself.*

## 1. After the Breaking, the Becoming

When the breaking was done
and the dust began to settle,
I realized the ruins
were not a grave
they were a clearing.

A place to rebuild.
A place to begin again.

*Becoming is not rebirth.*
*It is recognition.*

A remembering of what the ache
tried to erase:
your origin was always light.

## 2. The Shape of My Rising

My rising did not look
how I imagined.

It did not roar.
It did not blaze.
It did not tear the sky open.

It curled first
small, cautious,
like a hand learning
how to unclench.

Rising is not always upward.
Sometimes it is inward.
A gathering.
A reclaiming.
A slow, steady returning
to the truth of who you are.

This is the shape
my rising took:
quiet resilience,
soft certainty,
a kind of courage
that whispers instead of shouts.

### 3. What Love Makes Possible

Love is not only
what holds you
when the world collapses.

Love is also
what calls you
into the life
you are meant to inhabit.

It is the hand
that lifts your chin
toward the horizon,

the whisper that reminds you
you were made for more
than survival.

Love repairs
what breaking revealed.
Love builds
where grief cleared space.

Love makes possible
the life that waits
on the other side
of your becoming.

## 4. The Return of My Own Voice

For a long time,
I spoke in echoes
repeating the pain
that taught me how to breathe.

But one morning,
my voice returned.

Not loudly,
not suddenly
but like a soft chord
finding its way back
to the song
it was born to sing.

Trauma steals tone.
Healing restores timbre.
Belonging reshapes breath.

My voice came home
in pieces,
and I welcomed
every fragment.

## 5. I Am Learning the Language of Light

Light has its own vocabulary.

It speaks in openings,
in invitations,
in the warmth that gathers
at the edge of fear.

I am learning to read it
slowly,
like someone studying
a long-forgotten ancestral tongue.

Light does not demand.
It beckons.

And I am beginning
to understand
what it has been saying
all along.

## 6. What Remains After the Storm

After the storm,
I walked through the wreckage
of who I had been
and found seeds.

Tiny.
Unassuming.
Alive.

Grief uprooted me,
but it also cleared the ground.

And from that ground,
new roots learned
how to reach deeper
than the wind could touch.

What remains
is not what was destroyed
but what survived.

## 7. Becoming the Person My Grief Required

Grief demanded a version of me
I did not yet know how to be.

Someone steadier.
Someone softer.
Someone who could sit
with the ache
without collapsing beneath it.

So I grew.

Not perfectly.
Not gracefully.
But truly.

I became the person
my grief required
and the person
my becoming deserved.

## 8. A New Kind of Strength

Strength used to mean
holding everything together.

Now strength means
letting go
with both hands open.

Strength means
staying soft
in a world
that keeps offering reasons
to harden.

Strength means
choosing presence
over performance,

truth
over pretending,

growth
over certainty.

This is the strength
grief taught me.

## 9. The Opening That Saved Me

There was a single moment
small, quiet,
almost unremarkable
when something inside me opened.

Not a crack,
not a wound.
A window.

A place where breath entered
for the first time in months,
and the world
didn't feel impossible.

It wasn't dramatic.
It wasn't loud.
It wasn't miraculous.

But it saved me.
Because openings,
no matter how small,
always save us.

## 10. Becoming Requires Release

Becoming is a subtraction
before it is an addition.

The letting go
must come before
the letting in.

You cannot carry
what you were
and what you are becoming
at the same time.

Something must be set down.
Something must be forgiven.
Something must be released.

Only then
can you rise.

## 11. What I Owe Myself Now

I owe myself gentleness.
I owe myself truth.
I owe myself permission
to begin again
without apology.

I owe myself
the softness
I always reserved for others.

I owe myself
a life that feels like living
not performing,
not proving,
not enduring.

Becoming taught me this:
I am worthy
of my own tenderness.

## Micro-Epitaph—Fire · Becoming

You are not who you were.
You are what remains:
fire-tested,
wind-forged,
reborn.

## Reflection—Surrender · Identity · Alignment · Courage

- What part of you is ready to burn so something new can live?
- Which voices still echo in you that no longer belong to your becoming?
- How does forgiveness feel in your body when you stop fighting the past?
- Where in your life is ash becoming soil?
- What would it mean to belong to yourself without condition?

# MOVEMENT IV—HOMECOMING (Returning)

This is the movement of return
to breath,
to belonging,
to your own name.

If Movement I was the ache,
Movement II the listening,
Movement III the becoming,
then Movement IV is the homecoming:
the arrival
into the life your healing has made possible.

This is where you stand in the light
not as someone untouched by darkness,
but as someone shaped by it
into something whole.

## MOVEMENT IV OPENER

Homecoming is not a place.
It is a recognition.

A soft turning inward
toward the person
you have always been
beneath the debris of grief,
beneath the noise of fear,
beneath the expectations
that were never yours to carry.

Homecoming is the quiet truth:
You are not returning
to who you were.

You are returning
to who you are.

This is the movement
of liberation
a gentle, steady unfolding
of the self
you have waited your whole life
to meet.

## 1. The Long Return to Myself

I thought healing would take me
back to who I used to be.

Instead, it led me forward
to the person I was always meant
to grow into.

The return was not quick.
It was not easy.
It was not graceful.

But it was true.

With every breath,
I found a piece of myself
I didn't know had survived
the breaking.

And somewhere along the journey,
I realized:

I was not returning to the past
I was returning to myself.

## 2. I Am Ready to Be Seen Again

For a long time,
I lived behind my own shadow.

I hid in the quiet corners
where grief taught me
to disappear.

But now, something in me
has stepped forward
not loud,
not demanding,
just present.

I am ready
to be seen again.
Not as a performance,
but as a person.
Not as a survivor,
but as a soul
worth witnessing.

*This is what healing gives us:*
*the courage*
*to stand in our own light.*

## 3. What I Learned While Carrying the Light

Light is not an achievement.
It is a practice.

It flickers.
It steadies.
It falters.
It returns.

I learned that carrying the light
does not mean you are never afraid
only that you have chosen
not to abandon yourself
in the dark.

Light is not what saves us.
It is what sustains us
as we save ourselves.

## 4. Wholeness Is Not What I Expected

I thought wholeness meant
perfection
a polished, unbroken life
with no scars.

But wholeness arrived
looking nothing like that.

It came with seams,
with stories,
with a tenderness
crafted from the ache
that once unraveled me.

Wholeness is not the absence of wounds.
It is the presence of wisdom
the kind you can only learn
from learning how to mend.

## 5. The Horizon I Now Call Home

For years,
my horizon was shaped
by survival
the next breath,
the next step,
the next attempt
to hold myself together.

But now,
my horizon expands.
It widens with possibility.
It softens with hope.

The future no longer feels
like a place of fear.

It feels like a home
I am finally ready
to walk toward.

## 6. I Forgive the Person I Had to Become to Survive

I was not proud
of who I became
in the darkest season.

I shut down.
I withdrew.
I hardened
just to keep breathing.

But survival is not shameful.
It is sacred.

Today, I forgive the version of me
who held the world together
with trembling hands.

They carried me
when I had nothing left
but will.

They deserve my gratitude,
not my judgment.

## 7. The Softest Place to Land

After everything
every loss,
every unraveling,
every quiet night
when the world felt too heavy
I discovered something
I never expected:

The softest place to land
was inside myself.

Not in certainty.
Not in control.
Not in perfection.

But in presence.
In compassion.
In the gentle truth
that I am still here,
still becoming,
still capable
of beauty.

## 8. A New Story Begins

The ending you feared
was never the end.

It was a threshold.

A narrow passage
leading to a wider life.

You step forward now
not healed completely,
not fearless,
not flawless
but honest,
aligned,
and alive.

A new story begins
not when the past is fixed,
but when the future
is embraced
with an open heart.

## Micro-Epitaph—Homecoming · Beauty of What Remains

The storm ended.
We counted what stayed.
It was enough
and then, somehow,
it became everything.

## Reflection—Wholeness · Peace · Homecoming

- What did the storm take, and what did it give you room to keep?
- Where in your life do you need a longer table and a slower clock?
- Who are the quiet lights among you, and how will you honor them?
- Which door in you is always open, and what might walk through if you let it?
- If belonging began with one small act this week, what would it be?

## Acknowledgments

To my family, friends, and the communities that held me, thank you for carrying me through the seasons when I could not carry myself.

To every soul who trusted me with their own stories of grief, identity, and healing, your courage shaped these pages.

To those who sit with others in their darkest hours,
your work is sacred, needed, seen, and cherished.

Every word in this book carries the imprint of those who walked alongside me.

I am deeply grateful.

## About the Author

Barry C. Eneh is a public health scholar, healthcare chaplain, poet, and founder of the Sunward Institute, a meaning-centered initiative devoted to accompanying individuals and institutions through grief, identity, and transition.

For more than two decades, his work has unfolded at the intersection of narrative medicine, public health, trauma-informed care, and human dignity. He writes with a disciplined tenderness, helping readers live more honestly with loss, recover the integrity of their stories, and return—quietly, steadily—to the light that suffering does not extinguish.

He is the author of *Pulse of Becoming: The Path of Infinite Transformation*. *Tides That Shape Us* continues his ongoing body of work on becoming, grief, and renewal.

## Closing Note

Thank you for spending time with these words, and with your own heart.

May you leave these pages with more gentleness and compassion toward yourself, and with the quiet courage to keep becoming.

Remember: You are not what you lost.

You are what you are learning to rise into.

Go gently. Move toward the light.